Walking with us

Poems and prayers around the year

by
Daphne Kitching

Illustrations by
Elaine F. Hill

British Library Cataloguing in Publication Data.

A catalogue record for this book is available from the British Library.

ISBN 978-0-9932130-0-7

First published: Parish Pump Publishing 2015.

Distributed by: Parish Pump Ltd. PO Box 236, Macclesfield, Cheshire, UK SK10 4GJ.
E: enquiries@parishpump.co.uk W: www.parishpump.co.uk

Designed, printed and bound in Great Britain by EPrint, 13 Fenlake Business Centre, Peterborough PE1 5BQ www.riverdp.com

On the road to Emmaus

Now that same day two of them were going to a village called Emmaus, about seven miles from Jerusalem. They were talking with each other about everything that had happened. As they talked and discussed these things with each other, Jesus himself came up and walked along with them, but they were kept from recognising him…

and beginning with Moses and all the Prophets, he explained to them what was said in all the Scriptures concerning himself…

When he was at the table with them, he took bread, gave thanks, broke it and began to give it to them. Then their eyes were opened and they recognised him…

They returned at once to Jerusalem. They found the eleven and those with them, assembled together and saying, "It is true! The Lord has risen and has appeared to Simon." Then the two told what had happened on the way, and how Jesus was recognised by them when he broke the bread.

Luke 24 v13-16, 27, 30-31, 33-35

This book is dedicated

to David -

another man after the Lord's own heart,
and my great love and support, always.

Thank you.

1 Sam13:14

...and in memory of Anne.

Contents

JULY

AUGUST

SEPTEMBER

OCTOBER

NOVEMBER/DECEMBER

JANUARY

FEBRUARY

Walking with us

by Daphne Kitching

Poems and prayers around the church year – starting with Easter.

Introduction

Jesus is alive!

It might seem strange to start this book of poems around the year with the Easter-time selection, but I make no apology. Some might feel that such a book should start with Advent, the traditional beginning of the church's year. Others might expect January to be the logical starting point. But for me it has to be Easter. Without the resurrection of Jesus, there would be no Christian good news to share. Nothing makes sense without it.

The discovery that Jesus is alive, and not just a shadowy figure from an old text, changed my life. The reality that he walks with us, whether or not we are always aware of it, is the starting point for my book. The account of the risen Jesus meeting the disciples on the Road to Emmaus and opening their eyes through scripture(word) and the breaking of bread(sacrament) was significant in my own journey to ordination, so it seems appropriate to start the book with my resurrection poem, Emmaus.

Almost every poem is based on the scriptures that reveal Jesus and point to him. My prayer is that the poems will be useful in making Jesus Christ known in a world that so badly needs his message of love and salvation.

Starting with Easter isn't the only liberty I have taken with the year. To allow for the moveable date of Easter, I have grouped some months together so there are only nine sections not twelve. The March/April section includes Holy Week and Easter poems, May/June includes Pentecost poems, while November/December combines the Advent and Christmas selections. It shouldn't be too difficult to navigate. Some poems fit loosely into their months! Most are linked, in some way, to the Common Worship Lectionary structure and readings.

Many of these poems were written for the Parish Pump website. I would like to thank editor Anne Coomes for the wonderful resource that Parish Pump is, for her great encouragement of me over the years and most of all for enabling the poems to go further afield by publishing this book. Thanks also to Richard Vernon at Eprint for all his help and wisdom.

I thank Elaine Hill for the wonderful illustrations - and Revd Richard Hill for that request for a poem for Easter, one year, that started it all off.

I should also like to thank Bishop Richard Frith for his support and guidance in the ministry to which God has called me, and particularly for his encouragement of this ministry of poetry.

To God be the glory!

Daphne Kitching

Editor's note

Welcome to Daphne Kitching's poems.

It is with great pleasure that Parish Pump presents to you this book of poems by Daphne Kitching. Now you can enjoy them as much as her thousands of readers through Parish Pump do each month, from Australia to the Outer Hebrides!

Many years ago, when Parish Pump first decided it wanted to offer poems, we were faced with a major challenge: where could we find a poet who could meet the demands of the role? The poems had to be of professional standard, they had to reflect an authentic Christian pilgrimage, and they had to be written in time for publishing each and every month.

Then we met Daphne Kitching. Her poems are windows onto an inner life lived very close to Jesus Christ. In her hands, a single line of Scripture suddenly comes alive, as she tosses its words up to the light. Spun round, tossed back and forth, those words cascade down as poetry, becoming diamonds of meaning, each one radiating the light of God's grace.

There is joy in these poems, there is also pain. These are poems for the times in life when you dance for joy, as well as those times when your heart is breaking. These are poems which will enhance your life, as they have ours, here at Parish Pump.

We are delighted to share them with you now.

Anne Coomes
Editor, Parish Pump
March 2015

Foreword by Bishop Richard Frith

Daphne Kitching is a person of faith, warmth and sensitivity. It is these same qualities which shine from her poetry and make this collection of her writing such a joy to read.

I have found Daphne's poetry both personally enriching and eminently quotable.

She often uses unusual phrases which shed light on the bible's own imagery. So, Nicodemus describes Jesus as "truth teller, time giver, sign-man of God's kingdom", and can say, "And when I left him, the night was over."

Jesus on the cross is described in the searing suffocation, in the bearing of the whole world's filth.

Daphne is thought-provoking – We are a market-place generation; life is a Word-search – the Word itself searches; There's something odd about Christmas.

Some of the writing is comforting – let him lead you from the garden of your suffering.

Other poems are encouraging – knowing that you are loved, by the one who thought up the idea.

The writing is challenging – we are consumers, yes, but disciples?; come down from your tree.... be different....change your world.

These poems are an accurate expression of Daphne's own Christian discipleship and ministry. Thank God for the inspiration they give us.

Richard Frith, (Bishop of Hull 1998-2014)

MARCH and APRIL

Emmaus

Ride of the King – Palm Sunday

Judas

The Servant Girl (See also, Peter, from June)

Pilate

The Cross Road

Only Jesus

The Changing

Have you walked in the Garden

The Women

The Josephs (See also Mary, Mother from August)

How could we?

Headline

Him and Me

Prayer for Easter-time

Easter Morning

Easter Prayer

Letter to Joseph of Nazareth

Prayer looking forward

Mother and Son

Mother's Way – Mothering Sunday

What love is this?

Prayer for Families on Mothering Sunday

Job Description – Mothering Sunday. A children's poem but useful and popular

Emmaus

(Luke 24:13-32)

In the breaking of the bread
Our eyes were opened,
We knew him then.
The Lord was with us
In Emmaus,
There was no doubt.
He was alive and with us,
The scriptures made sense.
What a difference!

But thinking back
To that journey –
    To the grief that overwhelmed us,
    The discussions, disagreements
    And debilitating disappointment –
A different opening of the eyes,
We never were alone.
Before the word and bread,
Because of the word and bread
He was there,
He is here,
Always,
Walking with us.

Ride of the King

(Lk19:28-41, 23:21,34)

We waved palms
And welcomed him.
Even on a donkey
Jesus had majesty.

All our hopes,
The hopes of generations,
All our longings,
And our expectations –
Our expectations –
Poured upon him
Through palms and praises.

Hosanna, Hosanna,
Hosanna to the King
Who wept,
Knowing our weaknesses,
Knowing our frailty and lack of faith,
Knowing already our next cry,
"Crucify."

Father forgive us
For our knowing and not knowing
King Jesus.

Prayer

Father,

Forgive us when we don't understand; when we can't see the way forward; when we react inappropriately. Help us to trust you and stay loyal to you even when things don't work out as we had hoped. Amen

Judas

(Mt 26:17-25, 21:1-11, 22:39,27:8)

Surely not I, Rabbi?
I cannot call you Lord,
Not after the incident with that woman
And the ointment.

I've been with you
From the early days,
Waiting for you to act,
Waiting for you to prove yourself
In power.
And you came into the city
On a donkey,
You talk about love and serving,
When we need
A king to win victories.

Show me your love
Jesus
Show me your victory,

And I'll show you
Thirty pieces of silver
And a field of blood.

The Servant-girl

(Mk14:53-72, Mk.14:50, Isaiah 53:3)

It was all kicking off in the courtyard,
the courtyard of the house of Caiaphas,
where I work.

They dragged in the man from Nazareth,
took him into the house
to face the whole Council –
and those bought to give evidence.
I know half of them,
they'd say anything for a few pieces of silver.

He had no-one to defend him,
to speak or stand up for him.
Even his followers had forsaken him and fled.
His face full of sorrow,
but somehow, not for himself.
As I passed, he looked straight at me,
and I knew that sorrow was for me.

I wanted to stay with him,
but I had fires to feed in the courtyard.
And that's when I noticed him,
the one who'd been there that day in the Temple,
the one who had been with Jesus.
I was sure it was him, Peter, I think was his name,
here, now, just when his master needed him.

But he denied it.
He denied being one of them.
He denied knowing Jesus.

And then the cock crowed.

I remembered those eyes,
and I know
why Peter wept.

Pilate

(John 18:28 -19:16)

Soft, my hands,
A governor's hands,
Soft, yet stained with the washing,
The washing that history freeze-frames.

It wasn't my fault,
They chose - though I offered them
One way out after another.
I tried to release him,
But the crowds were against me,
Against him, who had done no wrong,
Who spoke only of Kingdom truth.

"What is truth?"

I looked into the face of Jesus -
And I washed my hands.
I washed my hands of him.

Now all I see are his hands,
Roughened with the work of the world,
Pierced and bleeding,
Reaching out, washing clean
All who will trust and receive him
Who suffered under Pontius Pilate.

The Cross Road

(Mt 27:32-56)

He chose.
He chose the cross road.
Darkness, desertion and desolation
Pierced him like the thorns on his chosen way.
In his broken, bleeding body,
Through the heat and dust and mockery,
Through the heaving crowds of feeble men
He stumbled with his death tree.
Up, up, up the steep and cruel high road
To the skull place of the outcast
Where the cross road had its end.
In the nailing and the piercing,
In the searing suffocation,
In the bearing of the whole world's filth
His cross road set me free.

Only Jesus

(John 19:17, 1:4)

Carrying the cross by himself
He went out.
Sent out,
Yet choosing to go.
Word of life,
Choosing death,
Knowing the end from the beginning,

Carrying the cross by himself
He went out.
The only one who could,
The only way he could,
He went out
To the Skull Place,
For me.

The Changing

Reflections of Mary, (Mark 16 v1-8)

Our eyes seeing the same mountains,
The gentle touching of our hands,
Simply breathing the same air,
Pleasures unrecognised till now,
Gone....
In the changing.

In the certainty of our grieving,
You surprise us, Lord,
You are not where we know that you should be.
In the moving of the stone, Lord,
You surprise us,
In our sorrow, we don't see your victory.
But you told us, Lord,
Prepared us for the changing,
In your grace, foretold the triumph of your death.
In the changing from despair to resurrection
You surprise us and transform us
By rebirth.

Our opened eyes can see beyond the mountains,
Now we're held forever in your arms,
The air we breathe is your life-giving Spirit,
Gloriously given.......
In the changing.

Have you walked in the garden?

(Mk14:33-34,42, Jn20:16)

Have you walked in the garden of desolation,
Do you know what it's like to fall down?
Have you trusted and shared and been rejected,
Has the broken heart within you turned to stone?
Have you known the pain of misinterpretation,
Of betrayal by the ones you knew as friends?
Have you pleaded that your nightmare might be lifted,
Just to waken to a night that never ends?
Have you walked in the garden of desolation?

Jesus walked in your garden.

Let him lead you from the garden of your suffering,
Let him show you to the place beyond the night.
He has overcome the darkness by his death upon the cross,
He has won for you his glorious Easter light.
There is life and joy within his resurrection,
There is freedom and forgiveness for the past,
Let him lead you in the garden of his triumph
As he calls your name and offers peace at last.
Let him lead you from the garden of your suffering.

The Women

(Lk23:49- 24:-11)

Mary of Magdala,
Joanna
And Mary, the mother of James,
Watched it all.
They watched the crucifixion of Jesus.

They had followed him,
Galilean hopefulness suspended
As they stood with his friends
At a distance,
And watched it all.

But they didn't give up,
These women.
They followed when Joseph
Laid their Lord in his tomb, cut in rock.

They took note.
They watched and they wondered,
Before leaving to rest,
Returning early on the first day
Of the week that re-launched the world.

Mary of Magdala,
Joanna
And Mary, the mother of James,
Were there.

Surprised by the stone,
Dazzled by angels,
Terrified by enormity,
Re-born by the reality of resurrection,
They were first in the telling.

The women of witness
Watched and then went,
And were part of it all.

The Josephs

(Luke 23:50-56)

It began and it ended
With a Joseph,
The life of Jesus.

One laid him in a manger,
The other laid him in a tomb.

One named him Jesus
And brought him up.
The other asked for Jesus,
And brought him down from the cross.

They were both men
Who stood firm
When life said, Run.

They both turned disappointment and despair
Into stepping stones of trust,
And walked on, as witnesses
That to God,
Darkness is a light switch.

How could we?

(Mt. 28:1-15)

The guards, they saw the angel,
And still they turned away.
They saw and feared and shook as dead
When the stone was rolled away.
How could they, who had seen so much,
Prefer the will of man?
I wouldn't, would I,
If I had seen a part of God's great plan?

And yet, how often I forget
All God has shown to me.
I choose to doubt, I trust the world
For my security.
Lord, I have known your faithfulness
When darkness filled my days,
I will trust your risen promise
That you'll be with me always.
Hallelujah!

Headline

(Lk 24, Jn20:11-18)

Jesus is alive!
He appeared to Simon,
To Cleopas and his companion,
To Mary and many more,
Eye witnesses
To the headline of history.

And they told their stories
Of promises and hope,
Of disappointment and despair,
The drag-net of death
Transformed by encounters
With the Lord of life.

Jesus is alive!
The headline stands today
As we live the kingdom script
In our generation.
And he transforms our stories
And compels the telling.

Him and me

(Jn21: Jn16:23)

In the end it's all about him and me,
And my relationship with him.

He fed me with fish,
Caught at his command,
He forgave me
For my denials and my doubt,

And he called me
To emulate his feeding and forgiving.
He called me to love him
And his sheep,
To feed them,
To make known his love.

But in the end it's really all about him and me,
And my relationship with him.

Never mind the others, he said,
In this world you will have trouble,
You will be persecuted
And criticised
And accused
And undermined,
But never mind,
Never mind,
Look up,
Be steadfast,
Never mind the others,

You … follow me.

Prayer for Easter-time

Dear Father,
Life can be difficult. Sometimes it feels as though the sun has stopped shining, just as it did on that first Good Friday. Sometimes it can feel as though we are stuck in the darkness and it seems impossible that the light will ever shine again.
And yet the reality is that Friday did move on, into the most glorious Sunday. The Son did rise - and his light shines on, transforming the darkest of times, holding out hope and peace and life to all who will turn and look into his face.
He is alive. He will help us.

Thank you Father, for Jesus.
Amen.

Easter Morning

(John 20:1-18)

Who is it you are looking for?
Who?

Mary,
Looking for her Lord,
Early in the morning,
While it was still dark,
Looking for Jesus,
Expecting his death-wrapped body,
Finding, instead, the stone of surprises and loss.

The men come and go,
But Mary stays and weeps
For the love of her Lord.
Looking, looking into the darkness,
She weeps.

Angels in white turn her to the light,
And the possibility of grace.

And in the speaking of her name, the world changes.
Mary.
Looking, looking no longer,
The Lord lives, gloriously,
For Mary.

He lives for all who look.

Who is it you are looking for?
Who?

Easter Prayer

Generous, loving Father,
How can we thank you for the precious gift of your Son Jesus; for his life of obedience and servant-hood; for his choosing to die that agonising death on a cruel cross, so that we can be forgiven; and most of all for his death-defeating resurrection on the first Easter morning and the gift of his Spirit to those who put their trust in him?
We can't possibly thank you adequately Lord, but we want to try.
Thank you, thank you Father, that Jesus, our Servant-King is alive, Lord of heaven and earth - and yet still serving us, so that we too can live and serve.
Help us to be your Easter people. Help us to live lives of faithful witness to the living Lord, empowered by your Holy Spirit, building, in all that we think, say or do for your kingdom to come.

Hallelujah!
Amen.

Letter to Joseph of Nazareth

(Mt 1:16, 18 –end,13: 55,Lk 1:48,)

Joseph,
son of Jacob,
descendant of Abraham,
carpenter of Nazareth,
who could have imagined
what you would be called to do?

Loving Mary,
pledged to the one
whom all generations would call blessed,
Joseph,
you responded to angelic advice
and continued to love,
even when you woke up to shocking reality.

Joseph,
you went forward in obedience and faith,
protecting and providing for
your Mary and her Son,
passing on your working skills.

Joseph,
often overlooked,
thank you
for teaching Jesus
how to do great things with wood.

Prayer looking forward

Dear Heavenly Father,
As we move forward from winter towards the promise of Spring, we thank you for your unfailing love for us, season after season, year after year.
Help us to remember that you, who have walked with us through dark nights and difficult days, perfectly understand all that we have to go through. Thank you for sending Jesus to die and rise again, so that we need never walk life's journey alone.
Lead us on Lord, and as we put our trust in Jesus, may we face each new day with courage, secure in your love and in the assurance that to you we are so precious. We are your children, lovingly made in your image. May we reflect your likeness more truly, as we grow in our faith day by day.

In Jesus name,
Amen.

Mother and Son (The Annunciation)

(Lk 1:26-38)

She was to carry the Son of God
To the world,
For the world;
To not be afraid;
Though ridiculed and rejected
To choose to trust and accept,
To serve and obey;
To step into the possibilities
Of God's power and purposes.
To believe.

He was to carry the sins
Of the world,
To forgive the world;
To not be afraid, but
Through love to cast out fear;
Though ridiculed and rejected
To choose to trust and accept,
To serve and obey;
To make possible God's power and purposes
For those who believe.

The angel announced
The son to the mother,
Knowing she would be
Mother to the son.

Mother's Way

(Lk 2:19,51)

You treasure those things,
Keep them safe in your heart,
Where did the years go?

Everything still so fresh…
The birth, those moments alone,
Your first looking
Into each other's love.

And the visitors
With their wonder and wisdom,
With their gifts and their gazing,
Everything still so fresh…

Then the growing years,
Baby into boy,
Into man,
Into joys and sorrows,
Into life away from your helping,
Yet you alone hold his history in your head.

You treasure those things,
Keep them safe in your heart,
Of course you do…

You are his mother.

What love is this?

(Jn19:25, 1 Jn 4:18)

Love to watch,
Love to care,
Love that for a lifetime
Is there,
Is there,
Never withdrawn,
Poured out through the years,
Standing through danger,
Casting out fear.
Love as near perfect,
Reflecting its source,
The love of a mother
Of course,
Of course,
The love of a mother,
Of course.

Near the cross of Jesus stood his mother...

Prayer for families on Mothering Sunday

Father,
You are love. If we had to draw you, we might draw one big heart overflowing with love in every direction. And Lord, as your much- loved children we want to reflect your characteristics. Thank you for those who do. Thank you especially at this time for mothers – and others who love and teach how to love. Thank you for the special relationships of love you make possible within families. And when those relationships go wrong, help us to reach out with a forgiveness that comes from knowing we are forgiven; with a love that comes from knowing we are loved. And how much you do love us! So much that you gave us Jesus, your only Son, so that by trusting in him, we could be in a right relationship with you. What a parent! What a family we belong to!

Thank you, in Jesus name,
Amen.

Job Description – a children's poem, useful for Mothering Sunday

A very special person
For a very special post.
Someone who knows how to cook,
(Especially beans on toast.)
Someone who can clean the house
And drive children to school,
And buy the food and clothes and shoes
And use most household tools.
A teacher of all subjects,
A referee of fights,
Who, as relief from boredom,
Is an "on call" nurse at night.
A hairdresser and swimming coach,
At ease with dogs and cats,
(And hamsters, rabbits, fish and snakes,
Stick insects, birds and rats!)
Has laundry skills, a taxi cab,
Makes costumes for school plays.
Who *never* goes off duty
And whom no one ever pays.

MAY and JUNE

Ascension
(Lk 24:44-53)

Scriptures fulfilled,
Minds opened,
We followed him to Bethany.
And there was joy in the blessing
Of our risen Lord,
Jesus, God on earth.

And in the blessing
Was the leaving,
And in the leaving
Was the blessing –
His Spirit of life and power
To witness to the world
Of our ascended Lord,
Jesus, man in heaven.

New Creation
(2 Corinthians 5 v16-6v3)

God thinks you into being,
Plans you,
Draws in all your details,
Every part intended to be
As you are.
The master of creation,
His loving preparation
Takes patient years
Of workmanship and waiting,
Until, at the exact
Time and day of his favour,
He looks at your black and white image.
Love looks at you,
And if you turn your eyes towards him,
Jesus Christ colours you in.

The Visit of Mary to Elizabeth

(Lk1:39-56)

Spirit of blessing and joy
How we sang.
How we shared,
How we marvelled
At the wonder of it all.

Three months we had
To prepare, to praise you,
To ponder in private.
Three months backstage,
Before the curtain of history went up.

Nicodemus

(Jn 3:1-17)

It was night
When I went to him,
Truth teller,
Time giver,
Sign-man of God's Kingdom.

It was night
When he spoke to me
As if I alone lived.
And he spoke of life,
Of birth and re-birth,
Of water and Spirit,
Of the Father's giving of the Son.

He spoke deep into my life,
And stirring from my centre
Believing began.
And when I left him
The night was over.

Life

(Jn6:68)

Life is not always fair, or kind.
Life batters,
People betray us, let us down,
Even those we trusted with our hearts and health.
Landscapes change,
Things we knew and understood
Are tossed in the air
To come down damaged and different.
It all seems too hard,
Too hard to bear.
And it isn't fair.

What then?
Give up, turn back,
Collapse and concentrate on the disintegration?
Or with Peter, look up and say,
"Lord, to whom shall we go?
You have the words of eternal life.
We believe and know that
You are the Holy One of God."

Life is not always fair, or kind.
That's why Jesus came

Prayer when life is difficult

**Proverbs 3:5*

Father,
There are times when we don't understand why things are as they are; why those children are hungry and homeless; why that person we prayed for died when they had so much still to live for; why that relationship broke down; why that accident happened to that lovely lady. There are times when we don't know how to pray, when we just don't know...
Help us, Lord, at such times, to remember what we ***do*** know; that you are our creator; that you love each one of us with the love of a perfect father; that you sent Jesus for just such times as these, to be our hope, to be our Saviour, to be with us always, in all circumstances. Help us to remember your goodness to us in the past, to trust that you are walking with us in the present and to have confidence in the future, because you alone hold it securely in your hands.
Remind us every day Lord to **trust in you with all our hearts and not to depend on our own understanding* – which is limited by our humanity. Thank you Father that we are your children and you do hear our prayers,

In Jesus' name, Amen.

When the Spirit Came

(Jn18:26, Jn 20:2, Jn 21:12, 15-17, Acts 1:8, 2)

I denied him,
Watched him die,
Despaired, then dared to hope
When Mary told of the tomb.
Oh, yes he died,
And oh, he rose again –
My Jesus,
Just as he said.

I saw him,
Ate with him
Early in the morning
That day on the shore.
He spoke of following and feeding,
He spoke of the Spirit,
Of waiting and witnessing.

And we did wait
When he left us.
We waited, in obedience this time,
In Jerusalem,

And the Spirit came.
In wind and in words,
In power and in praise,
In heavenly tongues of fire,
And then we witnessed,
Oh we witnessed to the world
Of our Lord Jesus –
When the Spirit came.

Spirit of God

(Gen 1:2,2 Tim 3:16, Mk 1:8, Acts 2 0)

Dancing with the Father
And the Son
In beginning the beginning,
You were there
Spirit of God,
Breath of life,
Creator.

Revealing words and wisdom
To prophets and apostles,
To scribes and editors,
You were there
In discernment,
Spirit of God,
Inspirer.

Filling with life and power,
With truth and courage,
Overwhelming with love and praise,
You were there
At Pentecost,
Spirit of God,
Enabler.

Longing to come,
To dance, to reveal,
To fill, to overwhelm,
To create and inspire and enable,
Spirit of God,
You are here
In fullness.

Baptise us.

Water *(John 7:37-39, Acts 2:17-21)*

Lord, my fountain,
Here each day, un-metred.
Supply me, I am thirsty.
Fill me, I believe.
Flow in sparkling streams
To refresh and rehydrate
The burnt out and the dry.

Eternal spring,
Spill out your living water,
Spill out your Spirit
On us all
In these days.

In those days *(Acts 1:1, 2:1-21)*

They spoke
In languages they did not know,
And their speaking,
Told by prophets long ago,
Woke up the word
Of prophesying daughters,
Of visions and dreams,
Of Spirit-life poured out
And promised
For such a time as this.

Violent wind, filling,
Tongues of fire, resting,
Signs of the gift,
Signs of the Spirit
Pouring out on all people,
Equipping, empowering
Those who call on his name,
Those who still call on his name,
To continue, in these last days,
All that Jesus began to do…

Sounds and Signs

(Acts 2:1-4)

Sounds and signs from heaven,
How to describe them?
    A roaring mighty windstorm -
    Tongues of fire -
Words are too weak,
Too one-dimensional.
We need the Lord's own linguist
To describe them
Through transformed lives.

Only when he fills us
Can we understand,
Only when he fills us
Can we pour out the joy,
The love and the laughter,
The power and the praise.
Only when he fills us
Can we speak and show.

Come Holy Spirit,
Transform us into
Sounds and signs from heaven.

Prayer for Pentecost

Loving, generous Father,
In your love you gave us Jesus – sent him out to bring us back to you. And when he had completed his work, by dying on the cross, rising again, and returning to you, you hadn't stopped giving. You gave us your Holy Spirit. You sent him at Pentecost and you send him today. Thank you Father.

Fill us with your Spirit Lord. Equip us with the gifts of your Spirit that we need to serve you. Ripen in us the fruit of your Spirit, so that our lives will be witnesses that you are alive today in this world; that you have the power to renew and restore broken hearts and lives and all creation.

Fill us with your Spirit Lord. Send us out in the Spirit's power to live and work for you, to make your difference today, for your glory.

Fill us with your Spirit Lord, we pray.

In Jesus name,
Amen.

Days to make a difference

(Mt 27:51, Lk 23:45, Acts 2)

On the day Jesus died
The sun stopped shining,
The earth shook,
The curtain of the Temple was torn in two,
The power of sin cancelled,
Death defeated.
What a difference that day made.

On the day Jesus rose
Stones rolled away.
In the opening of scripture
And in the breaking of bread
Eyes and hearts were opened
To life in all its fullness.
What a difference that day made.

And on the day of Pentecost
The Spirit came,
Empowering Peter and the others,
Present then - and promised to all who repent and believe,
The Spirit of Jesus!
And he comes to us now,
So that we can make a difference every day.

Holy Spirit, welcome.

This is the day *(Acts 2:1-21)*

This is the day,
This is the time
To call upon the name of the Lord.

Spirit breath,
And fire,
And words,
And power
Pouring from the Father and the Son.

Promises honoured,
Prophecies fulfilled,
A new spirit-fuelled sending
And revelation
Of God's reality.

This is the day,
This is the time
To call upon the name of the Lord.

Receive his Spirit
And go into all the world,
In his power,
Magnets
For Jesus.

Prayer at Pentecost

Dear Heavenly Father,
We all come from different places, a bit like that crowd on the first day of Pentecost. We are from different backgrounds, with different experiences that form us. I can't be just like somebody else and no one else can be just like me. Thank you for the gift of your Holy Spirit to speak and reveal your will to us in a way that is personal and unique. Help us to be open to receive Him every day. Please go on filling us with your Spirit Lord, that we might be effective witnesses to Jesus our Lord and Saviour.

In his name,
Amen.

John the Baptist

(Lk1:14-17, 44, 76-80, Mt 11:1-6, Jn1:34-36)

At the sound of Mary's greeting,
Unborn,
He leaps for joy.

Strong in the Spirit from birth.
What then is this child going to be?

A delight
And a cause of rejoicing,
The time of God's promise at hand.

A prophet
Preparing the people,
Preparing the way for The Way.

A voice
In wilderness warning,
Announcing the Word to the world.

A servant
Submissive and faith full,
Knowing Jesus as Lamb and as Lord.

Strong in the Spirit to death.

Peter

(Mt 26:71-75, John21:15-18)

I don't know the man.
I don't know him.
I don't know him.

But I did.
From the moment I turned to him,
That day by the Sea,
I knew him,
Knew he was the Lord.

I so wanted to serve him,
Speak for him,
Follow him,
Fish for him
Live and give my life for him
No matter what.

He is the Lord
And I let him down
Again and again and again.
I go on letting him down.

But Jesus,
Who knows the best and worst of me,
Who knows how I rush in and blurt out,
Mix and mess things,
Fail and fall asleep,
Who feels the agony of the denied one,
Understands the agony of the one who denies.

He is the Lord
And he forgives
Again and again and again.
He goes on forgiving.

Feed my lambs,
Take care of my sheep
Feed my sheep.

Paul *(Acts 9: 1-22)*

I baffled the Jews in the city,
I, Paul, of the murderous threats.
I came, not as they expected,
To take prisoner the People of the Way,
I came, instead, to convince people of the Way,
The Way
Who appeared to me in light,
Revealed truth to me in blindness,
Convicted and converted me
In answer to my question,
In a moment
On the road to Damascus.

Now to Gentiles, to kings and to Israel,
To generations with scales on their eyes,
I will prove, by the Spirit who fills me,
That Jesus is the Christ.

Planted in the love of the Father

Planted in the love of the Father
You can grow..., *(include name of baby to be baptised)
You can grow.

Watered by the spring of the Spirit
His fruit you'll show,
His fruit you'll show.

And when the sun scorches,
And the thorns threaten,
And the storms around life's garden blow -
Your roots will hold,
And hold secure,
Because you're planted in the love of the Father,

**name of baby,*
You are planted in the love of the Father.

Reflection on The Lord's Prayer

(Mt 6:1-18)

Our Father in heaven, please help us.
We, your children, learn slowly.
So often we say nothing when your name is mis-used.
Often our lives do not reflect your ways,
Mostly we do what we want on earth,
And this can make heaven unimaginable.

We expect so much more than we actually need each day.
Sometimes we think we don't need forgiveness,
Sometimes we think we are unforgivable,
And we forget that other people make these same errors of thinking.

When it comes to temptation, we find our own ways,
We are confused about what is and is not evil,
We are confused about deliverance,
We are confused...

And here is the wonder, the grace and the mystery,
That you know us completely,
Our failings, our secrets,
And love us forever and ever,
Amen.

Foundations

(Matthew 7:24-29)

What will happen to my house Lord,
Now that the rain is falling,
Now that the floods are rising,
Now that the wind is blowing
And beating, beating upon it?

Sunday by Sunday
I hear your Word
With interest,
With conflict,
With questions.
I hear your Word,
As I build my house.

But will it stand, Lord,
When the rain and the floods
And the winds challenge?
Are my foundations
Sunday-sand of hearing only,
Or daily- rock of hearing *and* doing your will,
Living your Word,
Strong in the storm?

Lord, Lord,
Help me to hear,
Move me to act.
Let my house stand.

Signs and Promises

(Mark 13:5-13, Rev 21:4,22:20)

The one who endures to the end will be saved.

Earthquakes, explosions,
Tsunamis and terror,
Nation rising against nation,
Dictators destroying their own,
Floods, famine,
Families in sewer-slums,
Persecution, opposition,
And the list goes on...

Signs all around of a broken world,
A warning world.

Send your Spirit, Lord,
Bring your healing,
Your compassion,
Bring your good news
To those who must endure.
Open eyes to see beyond disasters
To the one who saves
And will wipe away all tears.

Come Lord Jesus.

Centurion Faith *(Lk7:1-10)*

He heard,
He sent,
He asked,
Believing,
Actively trusting
That Jesus' word is enough.
Great faith!
Great result!
Jesus spoke power and healing
Into the situation.

And today
He speaks still,
If we come,
If we ask,
If we trust.
His word is enough.

Say the word, Lord,
Into our situations,
It is enough.

Prayer for faith in God

Heavenly Father,
When the world is wobbling and our lives spin out of our control, when everything seems wrong and we don't know how to put things right, give us the gift of faith: *believing* faith, *trusting* faith, *expectant* faith.
Faith to believe that Jesus is Lord, your Son and our Saviour, alive today.
Faith to transfer our trust from our own efforts, which are insufficient, to his achievement on the cross, which is all-sufficient, bringing forgiveness and reconciliation with you, our creator and loving Father.
And *expectant* faith, that in our trouble, in our helplessness, in our fear, you will hear our prayers and act; you will bring hope and healing, rest and resolution, for your kingdom glory and for our benefit and well-being.
In every circumstance of our lives, give us faith – in you, Sovereign Lord.

In the name of Jesus Christ.
Amen.

JULY

Thomas

(John 20: 19-31)

How could I
Be in the right place for so long,
And then miss the moment that matters?

It's unfair and unbearable.
It cannot be true,
And I will not
I will not believe it.

I will not
I will not believe second-hand.
My eyes need to see for themselves.

The faces of joy, the peace
And the knowing, separate us.
And I want what they have,
Oh, I want what they have.

But the doors are locked.

I turn and look up through my sadness,
And He is here.

He is here for me.
He is here because I need him
And he knows.

My Lord and my God.

Absence, Presence

(John 20: 24-30)

Thomas wasn't with them
When Jesus came.
He missed out on the peace, the joy
And that breathing of the Spirit
That united them -
And constructed a chasm between him and them.

So many ways to be absent,
So many circumstances to cause isolation,
So many kinds of chasm, today.

But breaking through locked doors
Is what Jesus still does.
Overcoming impossibilities
Is his speciality,
Being present with us and for us,
Always, everywhere,
Bringing his peace and life -
This is why Jesus came.

And to give us the assurance
To see with Thomas and to say,
My Lord and my God,
My Jesus,
My Saviour,

Thank you, thank you.

Prayer to stay connected

Heavenly Father,
Forgive us that we are all so busy. There are so many demands; so many expectations. Emails and Facebook demand instant replies and, if we're honest, they drain away our time as we try to keep in touch with everyone, whenever they contact us. We keep in touch with everyone who demands our attention, Lord, but often, in all the rush to communicate, we don't keep in touch with you, the greatest communicator of all. You communicated all we need to know by sending Jesus. He is your love in person. He makes it possible for us to know you by trusting in him. Thank you for pressing the send button that gave Jesus to us. Thank you that you will never switch off or close down. Help us to spend our precious time wisely and to stay connected to you.

In Jesus' name,
Amen.

The Difference *(Romans 12:2)*

So often
I can't wear the right clothes,
Speak the right words,
Fit the right mould,
Be the shape people want me to be,
Expect me to be,
Demand that I am,
To conform.

But you Lord
Accept me,
Release me,
Make it possible to be me,
Perfectly free
In your service,
Open for you
To transform.

Mary Magdalene *(Lk 24:13-35, Jn 20:10 -21:14)*

In the opening of scripture
And the breaking of the bread,

In the nail marks
And the wound in his side,

In the miraculous catch
And fish breakfast on the beach

They recognized him.

But for me,
My Lord said,
"Mary."

Martha, Lazarus and Mary
(Jn12:1-8)

Martha welcomed and worked hard
And worried about so many things,
Especially that Mary didn't.

Lazarus lived again and found fame,
And shared supper with the guest
Who called him from the grave.

But Mary...
Mary listened and sat at his feet,
And filled the house with fragrance
In anointing him.

Martha served,
Lazarus honoured,
But with her hair and her heart
Mary worshipped
The Lord.

Your will
(Romans 12:1-2)

Called
In love
By name,
To live my faith
As only I can,
To worship with my obedience
As only I can,
To serve in your freedom
As only I can,
To know your will
For me.

Prayer to know God's will

Loving Father,
You made us in your image. Our whole life is a process of transformation to become like you. And yet it is so difficult to know, to really know what you are calling us to do; how you want us to serve you. There are so many possibilities, so many roads we could choose. Which one has your signpost? Which one has the green light for us? The disciples faced the same dilemma, "What must we do to do the works God requires," they asked. And Jesus' answer was quite simple, "The work of God is this: to believe in the one he has sent."(Jn 6:28,29)
Lord help us to believe in Jesus, with a real, active, trusting faith and then to relax, knowing that if we do believe, everything, absolutely everything we do will be your work. Washing up, working in the office, preaching a sermon or preparing school dinners, we will be doing your work.

Thank you for showing us your way in your word.

In the name of Jesus,
Amen.

Consumers or Disciples?

(Mt 11:16-19)

To what can I compare this generation?
They are like children sitting in the market-places and calling to others:
We played a flute for you, and you did not dance;
We sang a dirge for you and you did not mourn.

We are a market-place generation.
Consumers devoted to pick and mix,
Café church, traditional church,
Fresh expressions, stale expressions,
Flute playing, dirge-singing
Dipping in and out,
Moving on,
Rejecting what doesn't please me, right now.

We are consumers, yes.
But disciples?
Life-long learners,
Committed to the Way,
Devoted to the Truth,
Experiencing the fullness of Life which is Jesus?
Prepared to endure to the end,
Being thankful in all circumstances,
Even when that involves a cross?
Are we really becoming
And making disciples?

God, who sent the flute-player
And the dirge-singer,
Give us wisdom.

James and John

(Mt 20:20-27, Mk3:17)

Brothers!
Squabbling,
Jostling for positions
Of prestige and power,
Wanting to be great,
Wanting people to know.
Certainly, ***Sons of Thunder.***

And their mother -
Fighting for them,
Proud and possessive,
Presenting her boys
Through a narrow, rose-tinted lens,
Wanting the best.

Lord, what can you do with us?
We understand so little
Of your ways,
Your kingdom values,
And still you call us,
Patiently you show and share.
In Kingly greatness
Of the topsy-turvy kind,
You give,
You serve,
You die.

Lord, forgive us.

Parables

(Mt 13: 1-51)

Secrets of the Kingdom
Shared in stories,
Stories of seeds and sowers,
Merchants and mustard seeds,
Treasure and nets let down in the lake.

Everyday stories,
Eternal truths.
Eyes and ears open, blessed to see and hear
The secrets only faith can access.

Lord, grow our faith into understanding
That speaks your kingdom message today,
New and fresh
In the parables of our lives.

Prayer of thanks

Lord Jesus,
Thank you for coming to live as one of us.
Thank you for telling those wonderful stories of everyday people and events,
which you filled with messages of truth and eternity.
Help us, Lord, to learn from your written Word
and to recognise you as the living Word - and our Saviour,
the only way to the Father.
In your name we pray, Lord Jesus,

Amen.

AUGUST

Mary, Mother

(Mt 13:55, Lk 1:46-48, Jn 19:25,Mt 27:54)

Isn't this the carpenter's son?
Oh yes,
He grew up handling hammers,
Knew all about nails,
Was familiar with hard, thirsty work.

He was always creative,
Could turn the most unpromising piece of wood
Into something beautiful.
By watching his father -
Doing what he saw him do -
He knew how to complete his work.

Now others pick up nails.

And I, whose soul glorifies the Lord,
Whose spirit rejoices in God my Saviour,
I, who all generations will called blessed,
Can only watch
My baby.

Yes, he is the carpenter's son.
And surely he is the Son of God,
And mine,
And mine.

The Slide

(Phil 4:13 and Ciara Tallulah!)

As I watch
She climbs the steps steadily,
Holding the handrail,
Her two-year old feet following each other
Rhythmically, unhesitatingly
To the platform at the top
Where she sits down
And freezes.
Holding tight to the sides,
Knees up, feet flat
She judders down a little way
Then looks up.
Her eyes meet my smile, my outstretched arms –
And she takes her hands off the edge of the slide,
Shooting forward with a squeal of delight,
Trusting the love she knows.

Lord, I have climbed so steadily,
I have come so far, in my own strength,
Holding on, holding back,
Sometimes freezing.
But I am your child,
Today I will lift my eyes
And meet your smile, your outstretched arms,
I will lift my juddering feet -
And take my hands off the edge of the slide
Released to ride, by your Spirit,
Into the freedom of your will,
Trusting the love I know.

Food

(John 6:1-14, Mt14:13-21)

On the farthest shore of the lake,
Where there was plenty of grass,
We sat down
With our problems and questions and longings.

Yes, we were hungry,
Hungry for hope.
We looked to Jesus for signs,
For healing,
For fulfilment,
And Jesus fed us.

One boy's bread and fish
Fed five thousand.
Food and lives transformed.

We watched and we wondered
As twelve baskets of leftovers were collected.
So much we couldn't understand,
But with Jesus nothing is wasted.

And the word went round.

Wave Walk

(Mt 14:22-33)

Between three and six in the morning
In the struggle with the storm
You are here,
Calming fear,
Saying "Come".

And in the coming,
Darkness disperses,
Heart and body leaps
In a wave-walk of wonder
And light-sparkling trust.

Lord, when my eyes waver from you,
When the strength of the storm overcomes me
And sinking seems certain,
Re-focus my vision,
That I might walk the waves
Held by your eyes of love.

Transfiguration

(Lk9:28-36)

Praying on the mountain top
We saw amazing things,
Moses and Elijah
And Jesus, in dazzling white, his face shining.
The Lawgiver, the Prophet
And the Lord.
Written Word, Spoken Word,
Living Word
In glorious splendour.
It was so good to be there,
On the mountain top.

Father, help us
When we are back down in the valley,
In the everyday muddle and mess,
To remember your voice,
To see through the clouds
To Jesus, the one you sent
To complete the Law and the Prophets.
Help us to rejoice in knowing your Son.
Tuned in by your Holy Spirit,
Help us to go on listening.

Request

(Lk 11:1b)

Well Lord God, here I am,
believing in you,
trusting in Jesus,
knowing that you sent your Spirit
to connect us.
But sometimes the signal seems weak,
As though I've wandered out of range.

Lord, I want to grow closer,
to hear your voice
and know your guidance
in the nitty-gritty
of the life you have given me.
I know it's been said before, Lord,
but please, teach me to pray.

Mary, a woman

(Lk1:26-38,46-55)

Mary, a woman
Carried Jesus
All those years ago.
Obedient to her calling,
In the "Yes" of her faith,
Mary carried Jesus.

Filled with the Spirit
She praised God
And sang of his glory,
His might and his power,
Of his faithfulness
In the past,
And his promise for the future.

Mary, a woman, carried Jesus
To the people.

Receive the body of our Lord Jesus Christ, which was given for you, and his blood which was shed for you. Eat and drink in remembrance that he died for you and feed on him in your hearts by faith with thanksgiving.

Holy is his name.

Prayer of thanks for Mary and others

Loving Father,

You called Mary to carry your Son into the world.
Thank you for her positive response to a calling which led her along an unknown path, where criticism and misunderstanding might well lie in wait.
Thank you that she stood firm and walked forward in obedience, trusting you to lead and protect her in her vocation.
May we respect the integrity of all who answer your call to bring Jesus to others, in different ways.

In the name of Jesus - and for his glory alone.
Amen.

SEPTEMBER

Harvest Field

(Lk10:2, Jn 4:35)

All around, confusion,
All around, helplessness,
People lost in the bad news of every day.
Longing for purpose,
Searching for security and significance
Here in the white field of our generation.

The harvest is still great,
The workers are still few,
But the Lord of the harvest
Is the same
Yesterday, today and forever,
And this is his field.
He planted, he will give growth
If we will be his workforce
And go out into the field - where he already is –
To gather the harvest
Of his kingdom compassion.

Lord of the harvest,
In your grace, we pray,
Send us.

Matthew and Me

(Matthew 9:9-13)

Here I am,
As I am,
As I have been,
Known.

And you see and you call,
Understanding all the tangles
And the turmoil,
Up to speed with all the details,

Still you call
Me
To wholeness.

Lifted by your word
I will obey,
I will follow you
Along the Kingdom path
To another rising.

Holy Cross Acrostic

(John 1:12 and 3:16)

Heaven's love gift
Outpoured,
Lifted high for
You and you and you…

Christ, Creator,
Rescuer, makes
Outrageous, once only
Special offer:
Salvation – free to all who come,
to all who will receive…

Sheep's Tale

(Luke 15:1-7)

I didn't know I was lost,
Just thought I'd try a new path,
Walk a different way for a while.
After all, the rest of the flock
Seemed so comfortable, so sure of themselves.
I'd sometimes felt alone
Even with the ninety-nine all around me.
Then there was my voice - always one bleat behind,
And just because I sat behind that particular bush
Where the ewes always congregate,
I got pushed to the edge of the flock.
So, yes, I'd strayed a bit,
But I wouldn't say I was lost exactly,
Just wandering.

That was until night fell,
And I fell
Deep into danger,
Far from the flock,
Lonely and yes, lost now
And wanting so much to go home,
Not knowing how,
Needing help,
And the night so dark.

Then out of darkness
His voice of light,
Searching,
His arms of rescue,
Saving,
His heart of love,
Rejoicing
Because he found me,
My Shepherd.

He came to look
For *me*.

Going back

(Luke 15:11-32)

Could I go back
After all this time,
After all I've done,
The places I've been,
The wild living
And the wasted years,
Could I go back?

Would they let me in,
Would he want me at all,
Is it possible even now
To turn round
And simply go home?

From the coming to my senses
Comes decision,
Comes a risking,
Comes a turning
And a danger of rejection, after all.

But when I'm still far off
And searching
The way beckons like a beacon -
And there he is,
Arms wide in welcome.
And he's running out
To bring me in
To the still place of the love
That is my Father and my home.

Reflection, after the storm

(Mk4:35-41)

"Let's go to the far side of the lake."

He was with us.
Although sleeping,
He was with us,
In our boat, in the storm.
Yes, we were afraid,
Yes, we woke him up,
And yes, he spoke words of power,
Demonstrated who he is
By a mighty act of power,
But we could have let him sleep,
We faithless ones.
He was with us.

We arrived on the far side of the lake,
Just as he had said.

Prayer in stormy times

(Mk4:35-41)

Lord when the storm rages,
When the wind and the waves seem as if they will overwhelm us,
Help us to know the stillness of your presence and your peace.
And even if you seem to be sleeping through our storm,
May that, in itself, be a reassurance that we are safe.
You are with us. You will not abandon ship.
You will bring us through any storm life throws at us.
We will reach the end of our journey
Safely in your company.
Thank you Lord,

In Jesus' name,
Amen.

Priorities

In a minute,
Later,
One day,
Maybe,
Soon.
I haven't time this morning,
Perhaps this afternoon.

We'll really do it sometime,
Next week,
Next month,
Next year.
Now I'd like to be with you,
That's strange,
There's no-one here.

Prayer about Priorities

(reflecting on Martha and Mary's encounter with Jesus in Luke 10:38-42)

Lord, we are all so busy. Life is full of demands and deadlines, each one urgent, or so it seems. We rush around trying to do everything, trying to please everyone and sometimes we miss what is really important – and don't realize until it's too late.
Remind us, Lord, that some opportunities don't come again. And that actually, we do have time. We have all the time of our lives, which you give to us. Help us to take our time and use it wisely, to choose to sit at your feet, like Mary, and listen to you; to seek you first, so that the rest of our life time will be in balance.

In Jesus name,
Amen

God-sign

(Isaiah 40:31)

So tired,
So weary,
That the beauty
Of the gold-framed clouds
Over the mountains by the loch,
This particular sunset
Releases the tears of weeks
And months and years,
Oh Lord, the pain and sadness of it all,
Why?
And after such discouragement,
What now?

Then, lifting my eyes,
He is there,
Soaring, majestic in his element,
An eagle!
Golden God-sign,
Reminder of the gift of free will.
And so, I choose –
To trust, expectantly, Lord,
That you will exchange my weakness for your strength.

I will soar and walk - and even run again,
By your grace and your Spirit,
For your glory.
I will.

Prayer for mountain-top eyes

Lord of all creation, please give me your eyes.
Mountains are majestic and beautiful, yet when I look at ground level, the mountain is all I can see; solid, impenetrable. But, from the summit, a wide new perspective unfolds.
Lord, help me. Lift me up, unblock my vision, give me mountain-top eyes - your eyes - to see beyond the mountain; to see the way forward.

In Jesus name,
Amen.

OCTOBER

Luke – 18 October

Zacchaeus – found only in Luke

Wordsearch – Bible Sunday

Sight

Spoken, Written, Living Word

Living Scripture

Prayer

Word of God

Prayer of thanks for the Bible

Word for the world

Prayer for direction

Luke

(Lk1:1-4, Acts 16:10)

To listen, to observe,
To draw up an account,
Having met those who knew him,
Lived with him,
Shared his man-God
Gospel-making days.
To investigate everything from the beginning,
To write a case history,
As from a patient,
Was fascinating and convincing
To a historian and physician
Like me.

But it was the Spirit
Who anointed my words with power
And my heart with healing joy -
Only by the Spirit's leading
Did "they" become "we",
Only by his re-creating Spirit,
Theophilus,
Did Jesus live for me.

Zacchaeus

(Luke 19:1-10)

I wanted to sit here
And watch him,
Just watch the man Jesus walk by.
Hidden by the leaves,
Hidden from the loathing of my lifestyle
I simply wanted to see him
From my tree.

As I searched for his face
He found mine,
Reached where I was and looked up,
Looked into the heart of my being,
And Jesus did not walk by,
He came to me,
He spoke to me,

A tree is not a hiding place, my friend,
Believe me.

Come down from your tree,
Come down and be different,
Come down and change your world,

Follow me.

Word-search

(John 1:1, Gen 1:1, Isaiah 55:11, Heb 4:12)

Life is a Word-search.
Think John, chapter one.
There will be distractions
In the search,
Interesting groups of letters,
Many in the wrong order.
Some even making sense,
In their own way.
Sometimes all is confusion,
A jumble.
The temptation is to give up.
It's all too much of a puzzle.
But those who search *will* find,
And once found,
The Word
Makes sense of the search.

Even if some round-the-edge words
Remain a mystery,
Once found,
The main Word, the central Word
Is the key that opens hearts.

And the Word *is*,
And will be,
And even in the beginning, was.

It has gone out and will not return empty,
But living and active
Will accomplish the purpose for which it was sent.

The Word itself searches.

So let us search,
Oh, search the Word.

Sight

(Lk.18: 35-43)

A commotion
And a crowd pushing past,
Pushing past – and me out of the way,
So what's new?

But somehow today
I need to stand up,
I need to see.

Jesus is here,
Jesus the healer,
Jesus in Jericho,

Have pity on me,
My eyes and my heart have been blind Lord,
Oh Jesus, please help me to see.

And there, in the road,
Jesus met me.
The light of the world switched on,
A gift for me
To follow.

Spoken, Written, Living Word

(Gen1:3+31, 3, Ps 119:105, Isaiah 40:8, 55:11, Jn1:1)

God has spoken.
His word created everything
In the beginning.
God saw all
That he had spoken into being,
And it was very good,
His spoken world.

He spoke freedom
To the ones in his image.
But then a stumbling
And a falling
And a need for the path to be lit.
By his power,
Through his people
It is written,
God's word.
To stand for ever,
To accomplish his purpose.

Spoken and written,
Revealing Jesus.
Word-man,
Word alive,
Life itself,
Gift-wrapped by his Spirit
And offered to all
Who will trust and receive
The rescue package,
And live the Word
In the world
Until he comes.

Living Scripture *(Jn5:36b-end, Ps 119:105)*

We go to church,
Study the scriptures -
Wonderful words in so many forms,
Historic, prophetic
Poetic and dignified,
But meaningless
Without the light of the Spirit
Who inspired them,
Light to bring revelation
Of the one who inhabits the words,
Who is the Word.

Lord, send us your Spirit,
Open our eyes,
Open your word
To truly be a lamp to our feet
And a light for our path,
Lord, show us Jesus
In every word,
That we might come to him
And have life.

Prayer for Bible Sunday *(John 5: 36a-end)*

Lord, thank you for the precious gift of your word to us,
to bring light to every situation,
guidance and comfort, hope and encouragement.
Just the right word, just when we need it.
Send your Holy Spirit
so that when we study your word
we will hear your voice and discern your will.
May we reflect your love.
May we shine for you, as we live each day in your service,
in thankfulness for Jesus,
who is the living Word
and our living Lord and Saviour,
Amen.

Word of God *(Rom15:4, Jn1:1)*

It teaches,
Encourages,
Holds out hope
And shines light
When days are dark
And the way unclear.

It guides,
Speaks life and power
Today,
As it has,
As it will
Forever.

God's word,
Spoken,
Written,
Pointing always
To the one who
Was in the beginning,
Co- author, co-creator,
Walking word,
Living word,
Jesus,
Word.

Prayer of thanks for the Bible

Thank you, Father, for the precious gift of the bible to guide us and to teach us. Thank you for the obedience of those who wrote the sixty-six books so long ago, and for the inspiration of your Holy Spirit who interprets them afresh for each generation, including ours. Thank you for the freedom we have to read your word today, and we ask for your help for those who don't have that freedom.
But most of all, thank you Father, that if we put our trust in Jesus, those black words on white paper jump into life and you reveal him to us more and more every day, again by your life-giving Spirit. Please show us, through your word, how to live lives that honour you and reflect your kingdom values.
In the name of the Living Word, Jesus.
Amen.

Word for the World

(Mt 24:32-35)

Changing seasons,
Changing world.
As leaves fade, fall
And are swept away,
So, everyday, lives are lost
In wars, in disasters.
Sons and daughters swept away
Before they have time to fade.
Broken lives,
Broken hopes and hearts.
Signs of a world without love,
Signs of a world without you, Lord.

And yet,
And yet,
You do not forget.
There is a still point,
A firm foundation
For all who will stop and receive.

Heaven and earth will pass away,
But God's word,
God's word alone
Will stand
Forever.

Wisdom, healing, reconciliation,
There, for the reaching out.

Lord have mercy.

Prayer for Direction

Heavenly Father,
The world is broken. So many lives are broken.
People don't know which way to turn, or who to go to for help.
And yet, you have provided everything we need.
You gave us Jesus, who is the Way to you.
Prompt us, by your Holy Spirit, to turn to him, instead of wandering aimlessly.
You gave us your written Word as a living guide book and manual for living in this world.
Open our eyes and hearts to receive your direction through it.
Thank you Father, for your unfailing love and provision for us.

In Jesus name,
Amen.

NOVEMBER and DECEMBER

Remembering

(1 Corinthians 11:24,25)

We remember, while we live,
We who breathed with them.
Photographs and anecdotes hold meaning now,
But our children's children will see only
Images in boxes,
Flat and far-away strangers.

And those who lived and loved,
Who fought and died,
And those who stayed at home and soldiered on
And bravely to their pillows cried,
Will we remember them, as November claims,
Or just the sadness of that list of names?

A different remembering there is,
A re-enactment, a continuing
Through past, present, and future of His gift.
Linking lives of faithful witness.
In this remembering we live, who believe,
Knowing the love poured out for us.

Christ died, is risen and will return,

Do this in remembrance of me
Do this in remembrance of me

We will eat,
We will drink,
Living our remembering in love
Until he comes.

Prayer for November

Heavenly Father,
In this month of long nights and dull days, we remember those we have known, those we have loved and lost recently. We ache and we cry, as individuals and as a nation.
We read the lists of names of those who died in wars that are now history. Few of us knew those brave ones as living people, and we realise that life is fleeting. We too will soon be just names on a list, or on someone's family tree. And we wonder what life means.
Help us, Lord, to switch our focus, from our limited, "now" view, to your unlimited and eternal bigger picture - and to be re-assured.
Thank you for sending Jesus to make sense of life, paradoxically, by his death on the cross. Thank you that through knowing him, we can know you. Our names will never be forgotten, because we shall live forever with you, if we to put our trust in Jesus.

Thank you Lord for remembering us.
Amen.

Teach the children to remember

(Deut 4:9b)

Teach them to your children
And to their children after them,
The things our eyes have seen
The things we remember
From our parents telling.

And as the anniversary of armistice comes round,
See again those sepia soldiers and their sweethearts,
Who lived and loved and longed for peace and home,
Watch today, as widows weep on News at Ten.

And in the hopelessness of history repeated
Let's teach our children
Of a different death,
Of one who overcame the world and death's destruction,
Who rose and lives
And opens up the way to peace.
Let's teach our children
To remember Jesus.

Prayer for Remembrance Time

Lord,
You are our loving Father and we come to you for comfort.
Hearts are breaking at this time, as we remember the effects of war throughout the years and still today. Help us Lord, to comfort those who have lost loved ones, those whose loved ones are in danger and those who feel bereft in any way. We know Lord, that there are many kinds of loss, many kinds of bereavement, many kinds of grief.
Help us to be comforters and peacemakers in all our relationships.
And when we feel lost and the pain seems too much to bear, help us to remember Jesus, who suffered and knows all about pain and loss. Help us to remember his promise that he will never leave us or forsake us.
Thank you that whatever our situation today, he is right in the middle of it with us, holding us close, wiping our tears, giving us hope.

Thank you Father for Jesus, who lights our way forward.
In his name,
Amen.

Sending

(Gen.1:1, Jn.1:1, Jn 20:21,22)

As it was in the beginning
Sending Lord,
Of your Son and your Spirit,
Of your people through generations,
Now, Lord, you send us
To where you already are,
Love-links
To the margins and the mainstream,
To the visible and the hidden needs
Of those in darkness.

As it was in the beginning Lord,
Speak the light
Of your word of truth.

Jesus,
Sent and sending,
Life and Light,
Switch us on
In the power of your Spirit,
That, sent, we might shine your presence
And bring glory to the Father
And to the Son
And to the Holy Spirit.
Part of your mission
As it was in the beginning.

Andrew

(Jn1:35-44, Jn6:8,9, Jn12:22)

People say I'm the quiet one,
A man of few words,
The brother in the background,
And it's true
I don't like a fuss.
But I know what's important,
I know truth when I see it,

I see it in him.

Knowing and seeing
God's promise in person,
Hearing his call,
What could I do
But share?

First Simon –
Who isn't quiet or in the background –
Simon first, of course,
Then the lad with the loaves
And later, those Greeks with their questions.

Not much to give, you may think,
Just a few words,
But words to change worlds,

Come to Jesus.

Next to you and lonely

(Mt 25:31-46)

Cups of tea and people,
People who do and who know.
People with purposeful expressions,
Their eyes searching beyond her, through her,
The invisible one.
She's next to you and she's lonely.

Smiles and one-way conversations,
With thoughts and eyes elsewhere,
Never noticing the masks of brightness
Hiding hurting children,
The tired ones,
Who are next to you and lonely.

And the makers of the cups of tea,
The knowers and the doers,
Those who smile and seem to have so much.
They too wear masks that hide their crying,
The together ones
Sit next to you and are lonely.

Advent Song *(Lk 21:28, Rev 1:7,8, 22:7)*

Lift up your heads
Prepare for the Promised One
The Promised One of God's people,
Hope-light of Israel
Shining through the dark years
To Bethlehem and beyond.

Light the candle of Hope.

Lift up your heads
Prepare for the Promised One
The Promised One of Prophets
Who foretell the Prince of the peace of hearts,
Heart-peace which transcends understanding
And shines through circumstances and generations.

Light the candle of Peace.

Lift up your heads
Prepare for the Promised One
The Promised One of John,
Baptizer, who taught the need for turning,
For forgiveness and receiving,
Who made ready the way for Love to live.

Light the candle of Love.

Lift up your heads
Prepare for the Promised One
The Promised One, magnified through Mary,
God-Man, gift,
Joy-bringer Jesus, to Jew and to Gentile,
Joy to the world without end.

Light the candle of Joy

Lift up your heads
Prepare for the Promised One,
The Promised One who is
Hope and Peace and Love and Joy,
Who lived and died and rose.
Stand, lift up your heads,
Worship the was, and is, and is to come King.

Watch, Wait

(Mk 13:31-37,Rev 21:3,4,22:20)

Help us to watch, Lord,
While we wait.
To watch as we serve you,
On the margins,
In the mainstream,
In the mix-up of this world.
Yet always preparing,
Building for your kingdom
Ready for your return.

Help us to respond, Lord,
To the signs,
While we wait.
Not demanding details,
But trusting your word,
Holding your promise
To wipe away tears and suffering
When you make all things new
On that day.

Help us Lord, oh help us
While we watch
In the darkness,
While we wait
Through the between times
For you
To come,
To be our God,
Our glorious, victorious King.

Come Lord Jesus.

Knowing Jesus

(Phil 3:7-11)

Knowing that he is alive,

Knowing you're not on your own,

Knowing you don't even have to buy one, to get this gift free,

Knowing the answer to that puzzled space inside,
Knowing that this was what was missing,

Knowing that you are acceptable - as you are,
You don't have to be good enough,

Knowing that God has a plan full of hope for you,

Knowing nothing's wasted, not even those desperate times,

Knowing that there is a solution to that problem,

Knowing you are safe, that you no longer need to be afraid,

Knowing that this time you won't be let down,
That this will last for ever, and keep on getting better,

Knowing that you are loved, by the one who thought up the idea,

Knowing now, that life has a purpose - and wanting to share it,

Knowing that death is a springboard,

This is knowing Jesus.

Rock-a-bye

(Luke 2:10-14)

Rock a bye baby
The world is your cradle,
The wind only blows
If you speak the word,
Angels will rock you
And sing to God's glory,
The message of peace
And goodwill shall be heard.

Rock a bye baby
The stars are your baubles,
Crafted by you
Then set into space,
Born into weakness
You travel beside us,
Showing us life
In your beautiful face.

Christmas Father

(Mt1:18- 2:24)

Working with wood
And loving Mary,
My plans for the future were simple.
They included
Nothing of dreams and angels,
Nothing of danger and wise men
Bringing gifts for a child
Who was not in my plan,
Yet who himself was a gift.
Not mine, yet uniquely mine, by grace.
Mine to accept, to protect,
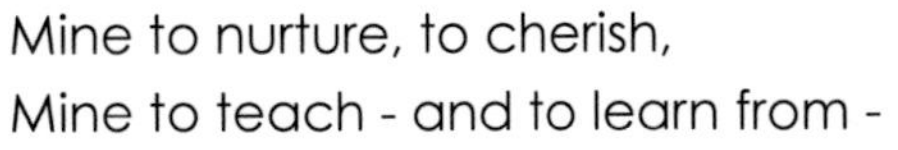
Mine to nurture, to cherish,
Mine to teach - and to learn from -
All that can be accomplished with wood
And love.

The Coming

(Mt 1:21-23)

Shops full of presents,
Diaries full of double bookings,
Days full of rushing
Round never-ending circles,
Evenings full of parties
And paracetamol,
Children full of media *must-have* demands.

Lives of tinsel
Hiding depression and debt,
Masking emptiness and insecurity,
Falsifying fears,
Disguising the darkness and dirt of our day -
As real as that of the stable,

And you come.

You come with your plan
And your presence.

You come to us,
Today.

Back to Front Christmas

There's something odd about Christmas,
In a back to front sort of way.
I can't help thinking that Christmas
Is a back to front sort of day.

We give presents to all of our family,
And people give presents to us,
But what have we done to deserve it
And why do we need such a fuss?

It's strange that the person whose birthday
Is the cause of this annual rave
Is often ignored, and not mentioned
On the cards and the presents we gave.

He's left out of his very own party,
No presents for Jesus today,
In the rush of our back to front Christmas
His presents are hidden away.

A "Thank you" would be a good present
For the treasure the poor shepherds found,
Just a moment to think about Jesus
Turns our back to front Christmas back round.

A Shepherd in need of an Angel

(Lk2:8-20)

He didn't want to be there,
He was cold and lonely and sad,
He hadn't chosen shepherding,
It was just the job he had.
He was a shepherd in need of an angel.

But because he was there, he saw them,
In a sky full of songs and of light,
Angels, who needed a listener
To share the good news of the night.
They were angels in need of a shepherd.

And after he'd been to the stable,
The reflection of love in his face,
There was peace and contentment in being
A shepherd and in the right place.
A shepherd so glad of the angels.

Christmas

(John1:1-14)

Fumbling around in a frenzy,
From September stress levels rise,
Dates collide,
Imagination falters
As presents and experiences fail to satisfy
The expectations of a world that walks
In the darkness of denial and discouragement.

Yet all the time
The light shines in that darkness,
All the time
The greatest gift shines on,
All the time
There is hope and life has purpose,

And with each turning to the light
Love switches on.
Christ comes.

Everyday Christmas

(Mal 4:2, Mt 1:23 and Anne)

Light a candle,
Look into the light,
Pray.

Light and life to all he brings,
Risen with healing in his wings

As the flame rises,
Smooth, bright,
Know the comfort of Christ
In the carol speaking
Afresh.
Bringing Jesus
Into heart and prayer.

Emmanuel, God with us.
Light of the world,
Out of the stable
Into our situations.

Because of Jesus
Christmas is everyday.

The Lord is here.
Hallelujah.

Christmas Presence

(Isa 9:6, 7:14)

Unto us a child is born
To us a son is given…

And you will call him Immanuel,
God with us.

Jesus, God actually with us.
God's greatest gift,
Born into weakness and vulnerability,
Sharing life's raw reality,
Family rows, family rejoicing,
Broken relationships, broken hearts,
Grief and great suffering,
Rejection and injustice,
Despair and death.

Yet through it all
Still the gift goes on
Revealing God's grace and power
And peace to overcome.
This is a gift that cannot be wrapped,
That will never break
Or pass its sell-by date.
This is Jesus,
The greatest gift.

Receive God's Christmas presence
And walk on with him.

Christmas Prayer

Dear Lord,
What's it really all about, this "season of celebration"?
People rushing everywhere, overspending, double-booking diaries in frantic attempts to meet the demands of a twenty-first century Christmas. And what about those who find Christmas anything but joyful – those who have lost loved ones, those who are old and alone and tired and longing for it all to be over? What's it really all about?
Lord, in the middle of the busy-ness and bustle, help us to remember that this is nothing new. Jesus came into a world of rush and frenetic activity. He came to a town so busy that there was no room for his family. And help us to remember that you know what it's like to have a loved one – your dear Son - away from home at Christmas.
Lord, still our hearts, and open them to recognise and receive your great gift to us. May we make room for Jesus and know the peace and security of his presence this Christmas. Help us to know that this is what it's really all about.

In the name of Jesus,
Amen.

Mission Love

(Isaiah 40:21, Gen 1, Jn1:1,12)

Don't you know,
Haven't you heard,
Haven't you been told,
Haven't you understood?

Well here it is then – some might say it was Mission impossible,
But truly - in the beginning, God created.
God, who is Love, spoke,
And by his Word everything came into being.
His Spirit breathed life into everything.
It was a good creation:
The light and the dark,
The day and the night,
The sky and the sea,
The plants and the trees,
The sun, the moon and the stars,
And all the living creatures of sea, air and land. ..
It was all good and blessed and in harmony.
It was a good creation.
And the pinnacle was the people,
People made in the image of their creator, to be in relationship with him,
Working partners, with the wonderful gift of free choice.
It was all good, very good.
Created by Love, Word and Spirit.
Too good to last some might say.
And of course it didn't .

Don't you know,
Haven't you heard,
Haven't you been told,
Haven't you understood?

Look around the world,
See evidence everywhere of the bad choices,
The broken images of those lost children of love.
Watch your television,

Mission Love cont...

(Isaiah 40:21, Gen 1, Jn1:1,12)

Go online,
Read your newspapers,
Walk your streets
And weep for the brokenness of that beautiful, good creation.

Mission impossible?
No.
God knows the end from the beginning,
He knows what we are like, what we need.
At just the right moment,
In just the right place,
In just the right way
Love once again speaks his living Word into the world.

Jesus, Word of God, made man,
Born to rescue, born to save,
Born to live, to die and to defeat death,
To rise - and to give new life by his Spirit
To all who will turn and trust.

Love, Word and Spirit.

This is a *new* creation.
This is Mission Necessary,
This is Mission Possible,
This is Mission from the Father reaching out
To all who will receive him, to those who will believe in his name, giving them the right to become his children.

In the beginning, in the middle and in the end, this is ***Mission Love***.

I have called *you* by name, you are mine.
Come to me.

JANUARY

New Year

Lord of the Years + New Year Prayer

Old and New

Wise Men – Epiphany 6 January

The Fourth Gift – Epiphany 6 January

The Baptism of Jesus - 9 January

Prayer of the Master – Week of prayer for Christian Unity

Work of Art

New Year

(Gal 3:29, Mt 28:20)

Jesus,
Heir of the promise,
Hope of the years,
You are here.

Help us Lord,
To know that you are there, too,
Before us
As you are behind us,
Already in the new moment,
The new day,
The new year.

Help us Lord
To delight in your company,
To walk your safe way,
To shine your clear light
Of hope for the year.

Reflection

Don't be afraid of tomorrow. God is already there.

Lord of the Years

(Mt28:20, Gen 1:1, Rev1:17)

In the beginning,
In the middle,
In the end,
He is.
Lord of all dimensions,
Past, present and future,
Knowing the end from the beginning,
He is our God.
His Spirit enfolds and enables,
As we walk into one more year.

Not knowing what it will hold,
Still we can walk on
Confident that we are kept
Safe by the Lord of all the years,
Who is our light and our way
And, most wonderful of all,
Our companion.

New Year Prayer

Sovereign Lord,
Here we are at the gateway of another year. A gateway we have to go through, leaving behind all the events and memories of the old year – all of that now known, and recorded, and part of our history.
Here we are, with no choice but to step out into the unknown, into the uncertainty of the future. But while we may not know *what* lies ahead, we thank you that we can know who lies ahead, if we put our trust in Jesus. He promises to be the Way, the Truth and the Life for all time.
Thank you that no matter what this New Year may bring, we do not move into it or through it alone. You are already there, as you were in the beginning.
So in this and every year we say, ***Glory to the Father and to the Son and to the Holy Spirit***, as we walk forward with confidence and in faith.

Amen.

Old and New

(2 Cor 5:17)

The old has gone,
The new has come.

What difference will it make?
A new year, a new day,
Same old me,
Muddling on,
Searching for meaning
In the mess that is life.
Always tired,
Always aware that something,
Something is missing.

Or, someone...

And Jesus says,
Come to me,
I will refresh you,
Come to me,
Receive forgiveness and peace,
Come to me,
This year – today,
Become a new creation
And live!

The old has gone,
The new has come.

Jesus makes the difference.

The Baptism of Jesus

(Mt 3:13-17; Mk1:9-11; Lk3:21-22; Jn1:31-34)

He came to John
In the Jordan
That day,
Jesus,
Man that he was,
Purer than the water that washed him.
In his Baptism
Man before God,
God before man.

He came to Jesus
In the Jordan
That day,
Spirit,
God that he is,
Affirming son-ship,
In a love
That asks painful questions
And answers with an empty tomb.

Reflection

By his baptism, Jesus completely identified himself with our sin and failure, although he himself didn't need to repent or be cleansed from sin.

Because he was fully man and fully God he was able to represent people to God, and God to people.

In his baptism he is acknowledged and affirmed by his father and the Holy Spirit. The knowledge that he was so loved by his Father must surely have sustained him through his ministry and suffering.

Prayer

Lord, help us to know that we are your children and that you love us and delight in us, and will sustain us too. In Jesus' name, Amen.

Wise Men

(Mt2:1-12, Jn14:6)

Once there were some wise men,
They didn't know the way,
But they were looking for it.
They followed the star.

They were scholars, they were searchers,
Who they didn't know the truth,
But they were looking for it.
They followed the star.

Although they were wise, they were puzzled,
They didn't know the meaning of life,
But they were looking for it.
They followed the star.

The star stopped over Jesus.

They were wise men
They were wise men looking for
The way, the truth and the meaning of life.
They found Jesus.

Reflection

Wise men and women still seek him. *Everyone* can come to the Father, through Jesus.

The Fourth Gift

(Mt 2:1-12)

The fourth gift they had was
Wisdom,
The one they needed for themselves
And the world.

Wisdom
To leave the familiar
In search of a new security
More precious than the gifts they gave.

Wisdom
To discover, in the starlit child,
A significance above
Gold, frankincense and myrrh.

Wisdom
And the eyes of faith
To receive God's showing
Of his Son.

The gifts we read about
Were three,
But the fourth gift they had was
Wisdom.

Prayer

Lord, give us wise and discerning hearts to tune in to you, so that we might serve you effectively. Lord, please give us that fourth gift - of wisdom.

Prayer of the Master (Week of prayer for Christian Unity)

(John17:13-26)

Spirit of joy
Oh, protect us,
As we work hand in hand
Through the world.

Sent by the Son
And the Father.
Fruit-bearers,
Called and commissioned.
Witnesses to the world
Of the Word that speaks
Hope into despair,
Wholeness into disintegration,
Forgiveness into fault.

Spirit of love
Overwhelm us,
That the world might believe
And be changed.

Activate the prayer of the Master,
Make us one.

Work of art

(Mt 6:25-34, Eph2:10, Gen1:27)

Clothing grass,
Fashioning feathers and flowers,
The master designer
Shows off his work to his people
In the greatest art exhibition of all.

His best work he keeps till last,
And invites us to look in a mirror.

FEBRUARY

Simeon – Candlemas/Presentation at the Temple, 2 February

Anna – Candlemas/Presentation at the Temple, 2 February

Waiting and Read +Prayer for Patience

True Love

Truth Encounter – Lent

Here to Worship – Lent – and/or when considering worship.

Stones

Wilderness

De-cluttering Prayer

Simeon

(Lk 2:25-35)

The waiting and the wondering are over,
He is here,
Revealed by the Spirit.

By the Spirit filled and led
I come,
With my own arms to hold him,
With my own eyes to know him,
Miniature of humanity,
Fullness of God.

My blessing a reality check
Of piercing and promise,
Of rising and falling,
To all people
In the challenge of light.

In the peace of my leaving, Lord,
And for your glory,
Let the light shine.

Anna *(Luke 2:36-38)*

All those years in the temple,
In waiting widowhood.
All those years
Worshipping, wondering,
What had it all been about?
Seven years of marriage
Then this lifetime alone,

And yet
There was this sense of purpose,
Of Spirit-significance
Impending,
Then there he was,
The child.
And Simeon sang
Of salvation and sorrow,
Of rising and falling,
Of light and loss,
Of revelation and piercing.

I gazed at the child,
Glimpsed the glory of God
And gave thanks
For the years.

Waiting and Ready *(Lk2:25-35)*

Waiting for fulfilment of a promise,
Waiting to see the longed-for light,
Waiting in devotion of a lifetime,
Simeon, trusting God to keep his word.

Ready for the prompting of the Spirit,
Ready for the revelation joy
Mixed with cross-shaped shadows of the future,
Simeon, holding Mary's God-filled boy.

Prayer for patience

Dear Father,
Waiting is so difficult. And we seem to have to do it so often, and in so many situations. Waiting for news, waiting for opportunities, waiting for test results, waiting for others – even waiting for you, Lord, when we so long for you to do something.
Please give us patience. Ripen in us that "patience" part of the fruit of your Holy Spirit, so that we can wait without anger, without frustration, without stress, knowing that you are Sovereign, that your timing is perfect.
Help us to recognise that, in the end, simply trusting you can take the weight out of the wait.
So help us to trust you, Father, and to relax in your care as we wait.

In the name of Jesus.
Amen.

True Love

(Lk2:22-35)

Broken world,
Broken lives,
Broken hearts
Without hope
Until there, in the Temple,
In that bundle of a baby,
Love provides
Restoration,
According to his word.

Truth Encounter

(Lk4:1-14, John 17:17,James 4:7)

Led by the Spirit
And tempted by the devil
He wandered in the wilderness,
Hungry
And focused on God,
And the truth and power of His Word.
Truth and power enough
To resist His enemy and ours.
To go on, armed with the Spirit,
To give his life,
To give us life.

A lesson in tactics then:
Know the truth,
Submit to God,
Resist the devil
And our wildernesses will blossom.
We will bear fruit,
Fruit to be known by
As his.

Here to Worship

(bearing in mind Mt 4:10)

First church member

I didn't like the hymns much,
Or those modern tunes, did you?
And as for Common Worship –
Give me 1662.

Second church member

This worship is so boring,
Rigid, staid, un-free,
Old hymns, old prayers, old everything,
So un-cool, so un-me.

Both members together

We really love you Father God,
And want to learn to love you more,
So, please, will you remind us
Who this Act of Worship's for?

Stones

(John 8:1-11)

Stones
Everywhere.
And so often we throw them,
Not taking time
To write on the ground,
To think, to reflect,
To recognise our haste.
To know that if justice prevailed
We too would have bruised heads and bodies.

Lord give us your wisdom,
Your compassion,
Your willingness to forgive,
To accept rather than accuse.

Lord, have mercy on us.
Help us to walk away from the
Stones.

Wilderness

(Mt 4:1,19, Jn 16:33)

Landscape of contrasts -
Wealth with want,
Celebrity with suffering,
Power with vulnerability.
A wilderness world
Without boundaries
Or signposts,
As secularisation sets in
And society fragments.
A technological super-world
Of cynicism and suicide.
A twenty-first century
Wilderness world

Then Jesus was led by the Spirit
Into the wilderness...

Here is one who understands,
Who is familiar with the landscape,
With hunger and homelessness,
With rejection and exploitation,
With temptation.
Here is one who exposed
The sham of self-sufficiency,
Who sacrificially overcame
The wilderness world -
And is still the Way out.

And Jesus says, "Follow me."

De-cluttering Prayer

Father,
Sometimes there is so much clutter and rubbish in our lives and in our hearts that we can't see where we are, or where we are going. We can't find our way and there is so little room for you to get through, to show us.
Help us to learn to de-clutter regularly; to sweep away the distractions; to throw out the things that take up the space we could share more wholesomely with you.
May we co-operate as you spring-clean our hearts Lord. Help us to make it easy for you to reach us, to sort us out and to fill each part of us with your cleansing Holy Spirit, so that your love will shine through our lives to draw others to you.
In Jesus' Name,
Amen.

Daphne Kitching is a children's poet, and a member of the National Association of Writers in Education. Her work is published in over sixty anthologies, including Whizz Bang Orang-Utang (OUP), The School Year Book (Macmillan), My First Oxford Book of Christmas Poems (OUP), The Works 2 (Macmillan), I Love You Football (Hodder Wayland), Cock-a doodle - Moo (OUP), Blood and Roses, British History in Poetry (Macmillan), 101 Favourite Poems – Poets pick their favourite poems (Collins), I Remember, I remember - a celebration of childhood in verse (Macmillan). Her Christmas play, Isn't he Beautiful was published by Scripture Union in the collection, Maximus Mouse's Christmas Card and other Christmas Plays. Daphne's children's poems are published in two collections of her own work: As long as there are trees (Kingston Press 2001) and Spider-flavoured Sausages (Hands Up Books 2004).

Since 2006 Daphne has been writing poems for the Parish Pump website and many of these appear in this new collection, Walking with us.

Daphne is a former primary school teacher and teacher of pupils with Specific Learning Difficulty (Dyslexia). She is an ordained minister in the Church of England serving as Associate Minister in a parish in the East Riding of Yorkshire.

Daphne is married to David. They have three children, James, John and Hannah and six wonderful grandchildren, Ciara, Jorge, Jasmine, Libby, Penelope, and Leo.